1

INTRODUCTION
Just Beginners

Although most of the rigs/traces are self explanatory they can be a little daunting to the beginner, this small chapter is here just to explain a few of the basic parts used in greater detail during the making of the rigs in this book.

Beads/Sequins

Beads are primarily used as stops, either side of a swivel on a pulley type rig or before a stop knot etc, one of the other uses for both is as an attractor on a hook length, these, used in the correct way can be deadly for flatfish etc.

Bait clips/Shield

Bait clips and shields are not a necessity but are a very useful item to add to most rigs, the clip basically slides on to the line when making the rig, these act like a small hook that you can clip your baited hook length on to and helps during the cast. When the weighted rig hits the sea bed the baited hook is released, these are held on the line by threading the line through the bait clip and then sliding the small piece of rubber tubing over the base of the clip.

Bait shields are slightly more expensive but do a better job during the cast and during the release of the bait, to use these on a rig you need to place the shield at the bottom of the rig before the lead link, slide a single bead up the line, thread the bait shield on followed by the small piece of rubber tubing and then tie the lead link to the end of the rig, unlike the bait clip this has to be semi fixed in place, to do this first attach your hook length complete with hook, when this has been done place the beak of the hook between the line and the bait shield, this action is only to hold the hook in place and not how the shield is normally used, now pull the bait shield down towards the lead link or clip until the hook length is tight, push the rubber tubing on to the bait shield at this point and with the small bead now sitting at the top of the shield tie a stop knot above the bead, once this has been done you have finished.

Lead clips/Snap links etc.

Lead links/clips are mainly used for attaching the chosen lead to the base of your rig, these enable the angler to quickly change the lead being used for another more suitable one depending on sea or weather conditions, these come in a range of sizes and should be matched to the weight being used.

Another use for the lead link/clip is to use it in the same way as you would use a snap link and that is attached to the swivel if used at the top of your rig/trace, again this enables the angler to quick change between rigs, these can all be replaced by split rings, however these tend to be hard to open with cold hands.

Swivels

Swivels are used to cut down the twist in rigs/traces during fishing as the weighted trace gets washed around

On the sea bed, there are quite a few different makes sizes and patterns of swivel and like the lead link they are all assigned to their own weight limit. Standard swivels are mainly used at the top and bottom of the rig or trace, three way swivels are used in the main body of the rig or trace and the free eye is used for the hook length attachment.

Care must be taken when choosing swivels, use the shockleader guide later on in the book to decide the size you require, but the average is around the size 4 to 1.

Zip slider/Booms

this is primarily used for making running ledgers, these can be used either from the beach or the rocks and are ideally suited for use in steady flowing estuaries.

The other main type of boom used from the shore, mostly from the rocks are the stand off boom and the pivot boom, these help to cut down on the hook length tangling up with the main body of the trace by holding the hook length away from the rest of the trace during the cast and whilst it is under the water.

4

RIG MAKING EQUIPMENT

Before you start to make your own rigs, there are a few useful tools that you may find helpful, these can be purchased from many angling shops and tool suppliers and best of all they do not cost the earth.

Nail/Line cutters

Nail cutters are probably the best tool to use for cutting line, particularly when trimming knots, the two types shown will both do the job, however the plier style are the easier to use particularly if you suffer with hand problems, the lever type will however trim knots that little bit closer.

Crimping Pliers

Crimping tools come in various shapes and sizes, however the ones needed for rig or trace making are the lighter domestic type, these can be found cheaply in some fishing shops, tool shops and internet outlets.

Using these is quite straight forward, however you may need to practice on a piece of scrap line, crimping it wrong here will result in snapping the line, crimping it wrongly on a finished rig or trace could mean loosing a fish and end tackle.

When using crimps first make sure that you use the correct one for the size of line, this will cut down on mistakes being made and it's a lot easier to crimp than an over sized one, below is a basic pair of crimping pliers.

don't be fooled in to thinking that using crimps is a quicker and easier way to make rigs and traces, it's not, you will use more materials like beads etc and you will make some rigs or traces using crimps that will just not be as strong as a tied rig, but don't get me wrong crimps do have their uses, it is almost impossible to tie a knot in wire trace line, this is where the crimps and tool comes out on top.

Hook Tier

Let me start by saying that this item is not normally found in the sea anglers tackle box, however what a lot of sea anglers do not realise is that these will work with the smaller sea fishing hooks, in fact these will quite happily tie a size 2/0 hook to 15lb breaking strain hook length.

The only thing you have to remember when using one of

these on a standard sea hook is that there is an eye at the top of the hook and not a spade, to combat this all you need to do is thread the hook length material through the eye before wrapping the line around the various parts of the hook tier. There are a number of different hook tiers on the market that all basically do the same job as the standard match hook tier shown below, these can be picked up for as little as £2.

Fly tying vise

A strange piece of equipment to have floating around a tackle box you may think, however when making some rigs or traces it would be great to have a spare hand just to hold that hook or swivel, this is where the fly tying vise can come in very handy.

One of the best uses for this is if you intend to tie your own feathers, however it is possible to use the above hook tier above to do the same job along with a rig making board.

Again fly tying vises come in a wide variety of shapes and sizes, however again it is the smaller one that you would need, either clamped on a bench or desk or the stick on variety will do the job.

7

DIY Rig/Trace Making Board:

A rig/Trace making board can be one of the best things that you ever manufacture and can be an indispensible piece of kit enabling you to make rigs and traces of all lengths and types whilst being held in position.

One of the easiest ways to make this is to first find an old plank of pine, like an old floor or skirting board approximately 36 inches in length and around 4 inches wide, the reason for pine or similar types of wood is that the pins used in this board are not fixed and can be moved between the holes, these will pull out and wear in chipboard etc.

Any way you have your board, now all you need is an electric or hand drill with a 2mm wood drill bit, drill a hole about 10mm deep at one end of the board about 25mm from the end and approximately in the centre, now leave a gap of 150mm and drill a line of holes about 20mm apart and 10mm deep all the way to the other end. Now drill a further two rows as shown below.

The pins used in this board are 2mm x 25mm round wire nails, this is the reason for the 2mm holes.

When finished use a pin to secure a 3 way swivel in the top hole, work out the length of trace you require and fix a swivel of lead link using a pin in a hole down the other end of the board, now tie a length of line between the two swivels held in place, this gives you the trace or rig body, now whilst this is still attached tie a hook length to the top swivel and work out how long you want the hook length to be, use a pin in one of the side holes to hold the hook whilst you tie it on, remember to use a bit of spit whilst tightening knots etc.

The items below are the main parts used for making the rigs featured on the following pages. Most of the parts on this page can be substituted for a similar type, Ball weights and Barrel weights are available in various sizes, the ball weight is mainly used for float fishing, the barrel is mainly used for spinning rigs.

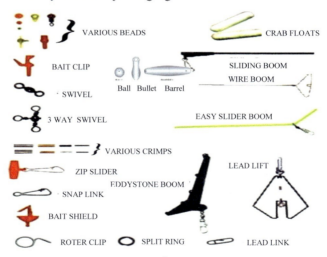

VARIOUS BEADS

CRAB FLOATS

BAIT CLIP

SLIDING BOOM

WIRE BOOM

Ball Bullet Barrel

SWIVEL

3 WAY SWIVEL

EASY SLIDER BOOM

VARIOUS CRIMPS

ZIP SLIDER

LEAD LIFT

EDDYSTONE BOOM

SNAP LINK

BAIT SHIELD

ROTER CLIP

SPLIT RING

LEAD LINK

RIGS INTRODUCTION

The main rule for making rigs or traces is that you use the same strength line for the main body as you have shockleader. For safety reasons this rule is printed below.

1oz lead = 10lbs strength line.
2oz lead = 20lbs strength line.
3oz lead = 30lbs strength line.
4oz lead = 40lbs strength line.
and so on.

There are a few items that you will need to build the rigs in this book, they are as follows:

* A spool of shockleader up to 60lbs
* An assortment of floats complete with weights.
* An assortment of hooks, sizes 2 - 6/0.
* beads large and small.
* An assortment of swivels, rolling and barrel, sizes 8 - 4.
* Bait shields or clips.
* Snap links, purchased complete with swivels.
* Crimps, these help to cut down the tying of knots.
* Material for making stop knots, e.g. power gum.
* Line for making hook lengths.
* Zip sliders or other booms.
* Lead lifts for rough ground fishing.

If you have followed this list then you should have enough materials to make the rigs, or variations of the same in this book. The art to making a good rig is to be able to tie a good knot and to tie the correct knot in the correct place, the use of crimps will work well on the right line, however if these are put on to tightly they can cut through the line, so although these may cut down on the tying of knots, these are not always practical.

The type of lead used with a rig is also very important, if you are fishing for flat fish it is best to use a dumpy lead as this will roll around the bottom and cover more ground, fishing a storm beach with a lot of current it is best to use a grip lead, this will hold the bottom and save the bait and weight from being washed onto the shore.

When fishing rock marks or places with a rocky bottom, the best weight to use is a plain lead possibly with a lead lift, this will help to retrieve the end tackle from rough ground. If the rig being used is for long distance fishing ,use a bait shield, this will help keep the bait intact during the cast.

Shockleader Knot

Tie a half hitch in the shockleader, now push the end of the main line through the loop and pull slightly up.

Now make a five loop UNI knot and using a little spit pull the two knots together and trim the ends.

Uni Knot

Push line through hook or swivel eye, pull 5 - 7 inches line through and make a loop, wrap through the loop 4 - 6 times. Now pull the line tight and trim end.

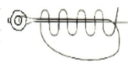

Tucked Half Blood Knot

Push the line through the hook loop, wrap around 4 - 6 times, push end of line through loop "A" and then loop "B", pull up tight and trim the end.

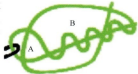

Clinch Knot

Push line through hook loop twice, wrap line around it's self 3 - 4 times, push back through first two loops, now pull up tight and trim ends.

Stop Knot

The stop knot is not used to attach anything to the line such as a hook or swivel, it is used basically as a stop for the float when used and foremost to set the depth that your bait will settle.

This can be made from 15lb line, however there is a  material made for this purpose called power gum, to tie this knot firstly set up your rod and reel with a float system, take a rough measurement of between eight and twelve feet and that is where you need to tie the knot.

First of all lay about eight inches of the power gum down the shockleader, then whilst holding one end about an inch in, take the other end and take it back towards the end being held so that you have a loop.

Now wrap the power gum around the shockleader and one side of the loop, you must do this at least four times but as many as eight, you must however wrap it around an even amount of times otherwise the knot will come undone.

Once this has been done moisten the knot and pull up tight, trim the ends and now this knot should be able to be adjusted up or down the line but will hold firm enough to fix the float depth.

Braided Knot

firstly thread the main line through the eye of the swivel and then follow the diagram over, but pass the braided line through the swivel twice. When finished trim the end of the line but leave about a 5 mm tag, you should end up with something similar to the picture over the page.

Rig tips

The number, and different variations of rigs used by sea anglers can often be bewildering to the novice or beginner. Ready made versions of many popular rigs can be purchased from most sea angling retailers, however, making up your own rigs, not only provides knowledge and experience but also immense satisfaction, they can also be repaired or rebuilt whilst out on a fishing trip.

The most basic of rigs are the Running ledger and the Paternoster designs, once mastered, these are the key to making the more complicated set - ups, however, bear in mind that the simple rigs are usually more trouble free and productive in most situations.

WEIGHT KEY OVER PAGE

1, Torpedo type lead, used mainly for distance casting.

2, Dumpy, this is used for fishing over clean sandy ground, where the weight can roll with the current.

3, Barrel lead, used mainly for spinning, however this can be used with a float system.

4, Pyramid weight, used for holding the bottom, over clean sandy ground. Not recommended for rock fishing.

5, Grip lead, Breakaway type, this lead is best used on beaches where there is a strong current. The wires can be set to break out easily if required.

General

Before starting to make any rigs, try tying a few practice knots. A third hand or a handy nail to hang the rig from as it is being made can simplify the process.

Use a pair of nail clippers for trimming end tags as these cut the line clean and close. When tying Paternoster rigs with bait clips or shields, try to use beads and crimps instead of 3 way swivels, totally build the rig, but do not crimp up the crimps until all is together complete with hook.

Now pull the swivel up the main body of the trace and crimp in place. this will make sure that the hook length is the correct size for the bait clip or shield. Never over tighten crimps as this can weaken or even cut through the line.

When using crimps to fix hooks to heavy snoods, loop the line through the hook and crimp twice for a stronger connection, it is best to use crimps when making up wire traces.

Snoods

The strength of a snoods is very important and should be selected to suit the tide and weight of fish being sought e.g. many anglers use a snood of 4 - 8lb, breaking strain when fishing for Mullet, snoods of between 80 and 200lb are commonly used when fishing for Conger eels.

The snood length, can also be of great importance for example, Cod tend to take a bait more easily if the snood length is between 24 and 40 inches. One of the best rigs for this is the up and over, or the beach Cod rig as the length of the snood can be tremendously varied.

Bass can react in the same way, however, many are taken on running ledgers or plugs. If making Whiting or Mackerel traces it is best to have a snood of between 6 and 9inches.

When making snoods, try to use a line which is not prone to tangle or twist, a good example of this is "Amnesia" (this is available in various sizes). In many cases other than heavy rock fishing it is best to use a snood length that is a lighter breaking strain to the main line that you have on your reels, this is so that if your hook gets stuck in any underwater snags you are more likely to loose just the snood length.

When making separate snood lengths it is best to attach a

small swivel and clip to one end as this makes it easier to change snoods quickly, one example is using a snood suitable for a Dogfish for a period of time and then changing it for a beaded snood for flatfish.

This method works very well when scrambling over rocks or covering a lot of ground on the coast paths.

TRACES

When making traces the shockleader rule applies as the trace has to withstand the full casting weight of the lead. The body of the trace includes all of the main line from the top swivel to the bottom, at the lead link.

When making traces from this book, there may be a necessity to use crimps, these should be put on with care and only crimped with enough force to slightly close the crimp on to the line, if to much force is used, the crimp can and probably will cut through the line.

If you do not feel confident enough to use these, or cannot acquire these, there is an alternative, this is a stop knot or, a piece of old telephone wire coiled, tightly around the line will work in the same way as a crimp or stop knot, these are adjustable.

Many of the traces shown are for use at marks that have more than enough room to swing a lead out from the end of the rod, for long distance casting, however many of these traces can be considered dangerous if used in areas with little room. For confined areas there are shorter traces, use these.

Making your first simple rig

After reading the first few pages you should have gained a basic knowledge of rigs and the components used, now follow this simple set of instructions and make your first rig, a single paternoster with a bait shield, note the bait shield is optional.

You will need the following parts:

1, snap link, 1 lead link,
2 x swivels, 1x 3 way swivel, 1 bait shield optional, 1 x bead, 1 x crimp,2 x 18" shockleader material, 1 x 14" hook length material, 1 x hook.

First of all connect the snap & lead links one to each swivel, now tie the free end of each swivel using a clinch knot to the 2 lengths of shockleader material, you should now have 2 swivels with links attached to the 2 shockleader lengths.

Attach the 3 way swivel to the free end of the shockleader on the swivel with the snap link.

Now feed the free end of the other shockleader through the rubber tubing and bait shield if used, make sure that the shield is the correct way up i.e. the cone is facing the lead link end, now slide on the bead followed by the crimp and let it run freely down the line DO NOT squash the crimp at this time, tie the free end of the shock leader to the other side of the 3 way swivel.

It should now look like the picture on the right.

If you are using a trace making board stretch out the trace between two pins so that it is taught, this will make it easier to set the hook length. All you should have left at this point is the hook and the hook length material, now attach the two with a clinch knot and then making sure that the hook length is now shorter than the distance between the 3 way swivel and the lead link, attach the length to the 3 way swivel. If used push the rubber tubing up on to the bottom of the bait shield, put the hook in place so that the hook length is taught, let the bead slide down to the top of the shield and then squash the crimp up behind the bead. There you have it your first rig and remember practice makes perfect.

Basic MPD Anti-tangle float end tackle

This is a very simple and effective piece of end tackle and as long as you keep the hook length shorter than the rig body, it is 99.9% tangle free, using this with a sliding float can also greatly increase your casting distance.

The parts needed for this are as follows:

18" Shockleader material, two medium barrel swivels, four beads and two short bits of silicon rubber tubing, this acts as a type of shock absorber during the cast.

Use this by feeding a bead up the main line followed by the float and bead then attach this to the main line and a hook length of about 12"16" long to the other end of rig body.

INLINE SLIDING FLOAT

This basic system of float is mainly used for long distance casting for Mackerel, Pollack, Garfish, Scad, Whiting, Bass and Wrasse. The above float is available in various sizes from local tackle dealers. Use float system on suitable size shockleader.

PARTS LIST

1 Sliding Float. 1 Ball weight to suit. 2 Beads. 1 Swivel.
1 Hook , size 1 to 2/0. 1 Rubber Stop Knot.

SLIDING FLOAT

Unlike the first float system, this one is mainly used for closer fishing for Wrasse, Pollack, Mackerel, Scad, Bass and Garfish. It can be very difficult to cast this system any great distance without it getting tangled. Use float system on suitable shockleader.

PARTS LIST

1 Sliding Float, 1 Ball weight to suit. 2 Beads. 1 Swivel.
1 hook , Size 1 to 3/0. 1 Rubber Stop Knot.

20

SELF COCKING FIXED FLOAT

This float is ideal for shallow fishing, and is a very simple float to set up, particularly good for younger anglers. A good float for Garfish and Mackerel. Tie the end of shockleader directly to the top of the three way swivel incorporated in the float.

PARTS LIST

1 Self Cocking Fixed Float as Above. 1 Length of hook snood, Approx. 6 - 8 feet, 1 x size 1 to 2/0 hook.

SELF COCKING MULLET FLOAT

This Float system is used mainly for light float fishing for Mullet ,although it is also very common in the fresh water tackle box. The float depth can be adjusted by pulling the line through the holes provided, best fished in calm weather with a depth of around 12 feet. This float goes straight on to the main line.

PARTS LIST

1 Mullet Float. 2 - 4 "BB" Lead Shot. 1 Hook Size 10- 6. 1 Hook Size 6 to 8.

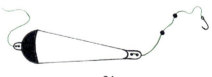

BASIC MULLET RIG

This is one of the most basic rigs/ end tackle to set up, you need no Shockleader, no hook length material, nor the use of beads or swivels, you just simply take a measurement of about 18" from the end of the main line, then form a loop of about 6" diameter, tie this in a tucked half blood knot so that you now have a loop of line tied in the main line approximately 18" from the end.

Now attach a small 1/2 — 1oz lead to the bottom end, once this is done, cut one side of the loop near to the knot, this should now leave you with a single hook length of approximately 12" attach a small hook i.e. size 6 or 8 and that's the rig finished.

Please note in the illustration green line has been used, this is solely so that it can be seen, when making this set up it is better to use either clear, ghost, chameleon or grey line as the species this is primarily used for tend to get spooked very easily.

This piece of end tackle can also be adapted to catch Wrasse etc. many anglers use a heavy main line for catching this species and therefore do not have to attach a Shockleader to the end of the main line.

22

In this case if using up to 25lb line then follow the steps to make the basic Mullet rig but make the loop about 12" diameter and don't cut it, instead feed the end of the loop through the eye of a size 3/0—4/0 hook and then push the end of the hook through the end of the loop as it comes through the eye, this fastens the hook without the need to tie a knot.

Attach a weight to the end of the main line, this will work the same as a rotten bottom.

RUNNING LEDGER

This rig can be very versatile, catching most species of fish, particularly good for flatfish, Bass, Cod and Gurnard. This rig is made on the shockleader, this gives the fish a long length of line to run with, before the lead strikes out of the bottom.

PARTS LIST

⇒   1 Zip Slider, with clip. 2 Beads.
⇒   1 Medium Swivel.
⇒   1 Hook, Various sizes to suit .
⇒   1 x 24 inches of Hook Length.

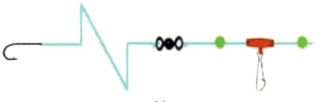

TWIN RUNNING LEDGER

This running ledger rig is similar to the first, however this can be more effective used with worm baits in estuaries for flatfish. Tie trace directly to the end of the shockleader.

PARTS LIST

⇒   1 Zip Slider. 1 Three Way Swivel.

⇒   2 Beads for trace & 6+ for Hook Lengths.

⇒   2 x Hook Lengths 12 inches & 24 inches.

⇒   2 Hooks Sizes 1/0 - 2/0.

PATERNOSTER SINGLE

This rig is one of the simplest ones to make and use, best for gentle casting, this rig catches most species of fish. The rig is tied directly to the end of the shockleader, by using the three way swivel at the top of the rig.

PARTS LIST

⇒   1 Three Way Swivel.

⇒   8 - 18 inches Hook Length.

⇒   24 inches Shockleader.

⇒   1 Hook, Size 1/0 - 6/0.

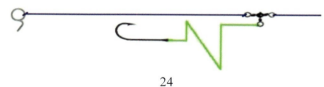

PATERNOSTER TWIN

This rig is slightly more complicated than the single paternoster, however this rig has the added advantage of having two hooks, these can be different sizes and be baited with different baits.

PARTS LIST

⇒   2 x Three way swivels.
⇒   2 x Hook Lengths 8-13 inches.
⇒   2 x 14 inches of Shockleader.
⇒   2 x Hooks, Size 1/0-6/0. 1 Lead Clip.

ONE UP ONE DOWN

This rig can be used for attracting more than one species of fish, it is best to use a plane lead with this system. this rig is mainly used for close to medium casting for most fish.

PARTS LIST

⇒   2 x Three Way Swivels.
⇒   1 Lead Clip. 1 Hook Length 12".
⇒   1 Length of Shockleader 18"
⇒   1 Hook Length   12" +.
⇒   2 Hooks Various Sizes.

WHITING RIG

Although this rig is primarily a rig for catching Whiting, it can be adapted for many forms of fishing. This trace is connected to the shockleader by the three way swivel at the top of the trace.

PARTS LIST

⇒   3 X Three Way swivels.
⇒   3 x 10-18" Shockleader.
⇒   1 x Lead Clip.
⇒   3 x 8-12 " Hook Length.
⇒   3 x Hook, Size 1/0-4/0.

PULLEY RIG

This rig can be made at any length that you are comfortable casting with. If made with a long hook length and body this rig is ideal for Cod, Coalfish, Pollack and Bass, and a short body and hook length for Mackerel, Scad and whiting.

PARTS LIST

⇒   14-30" Of Shockleader. 2 x Beads.
⇒   2 x Medium Swivels. 1 Rotor Clip.
⇒   1 Hook, Size 2/0-6/0. 12-18" Hook Length.

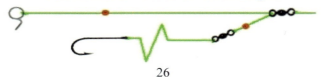

WISHBONE PULLEY RIG

This rig is similar to the first pulley rig, however, having two hooks can help if the fishing is slow, if you use two different sized hooks and baits, the chances are that you may contact more than one species of fish.

PARTS LIST
⇒   14-30" of Shockleader. 2 x Beads.
⇒   2 x Medium swivels. 1 Rotor Clip.
⇒   2 x Hooks, Size 2/0-6/0. 2 x 12-18" Hook Lengths.

RUNNING PATERNOSTER

This rig can be very effective for short range beach or rock fishing. Used for Rays, Bass, Dogfish, Cod, Whiting, Pollack and Coalfish. If beads are added to the hook length, this rig will work for most flatfish.

PARTS LIST
⇒   24" Of Shockleader. 2 x Medium Swivels.
⇒   2 x Beads. 1 Zip Slider. 12-20" Hook Length.
⇒   1 Hook, Size 3/0-5/0.

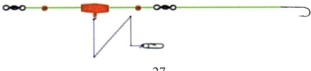

BEACH COD RIG

This can be a very versatile rig, mainly used for Cod, by varying the hook size this rig can be used for Bass, Whiting, Pollack, Coalfish, dogfish and will also catch a variety of flatfish with small hooks.

Attach to main line with a loop and clip or swivel.

PARTS LIST

⇒ 1 Relay Clip. 1 Rotor Clip. 1 Medium Swivel.
⇒ 2 x Beads. 2 x Crimps. 24" of Shockleader.
⇒ 36" Hook Length. 1 Hook, Size 2/0- 6/0.

WISHBONE PATERNOSTER

A good rig for catching Bass, cod, Pollack etc, for the medium distance caster, from the beach or rocks, this rig is ideal for use with larger baits.

This rig can be Attached to the main line with a loop and clip or a swivel.

The rotor clip can be substituted with a bait shield, this will help for longer distance casting, as with most rigs, replacing the rotor clip with a bait shield will increase the ability to cast the bait further.

28

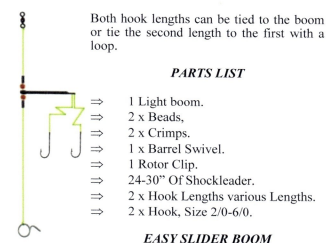

Both hook lengths can be tied to the boom or tie the second length to the first with a loop.

PARTS LIST

⇒ 1 Light boom.
⇒ 2 x Beads,
⇒ 2 x Crimps.
⇒ 1 x Barrel Swivel.
⇒ 1 Rotor Clip.
⇒ 24-30" Of Shockleader.
⇒ 2 x Hook Lengths various Lengths.
⇒ 2 x Hook, Size 2/0-6/0.

EASY SLIDER BOOM

This can be a very tough rig, used for heavy rock fishing for Wrasse, Cod, Conger Eels and Rockling. This rig is best used at close or medium range.

The Pennel hook on this rig is an option and single hooks work just as well. This rig is designed to run up the shockleader.

PARTS LIST

⇒ 1 Easy Slider Boom.
⇒ 1 Bead.
⇒ 1 Swivel (Heavy).
⇒ 1 Hook, Size 2/0-3/0.
⇒ 1 Hook, 4/0 to 6/0.

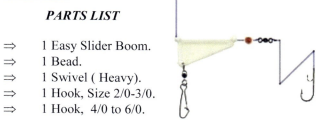

29

BOMBER RIG

This rig, with a few alterations can make a very good distance casting rig, for putting two medium sized baits out in the same area. various hook sizes can be used.

PARTS LIST

⇒   2 x 12 to 24" Of shockleader. 1 x Medium Swivel.
⇒   2 x 3 way swivels. 1x Crimp. 1 x bead
⇒   1 x Bait Shield & 1 x bait clip.
⇒   2 Snoods 1@ 10" 1@ 14". 2 x Hook, Size 2/0-5/0.

ROTTEN BOTTOM RIG

This rig is used for fishing close in to the edge over very rough ground where end tackle losses can be high. An old spark plug is shown, however nuts, bolts etc can be used. Main uses are for Wrasse and Rockling, although this rig can be used for any species.

PARTS LIST

⇒   1 Three Way Swivel. 12 -20" Hook Length.
⇒   1 Hook, Size 1/0-6/0.
⇒   18-24" of line, lighter than that of the hook length for Rotten Bottom.

UP & OVER RIG

This rig is a good all rounder particularly in a strong flowing tide or estuary where keeping the bait close to the bottom can be a great advantage.

This can be made to any length from 12" right up to 48" or what you are comfortable casting, and remember on a 48" trace the hook length would be in excess of seven feet in length, ideal for keeping the bait away from the weighted rig/trace body.

It is not recommended to use this rig/trace from high rock marks unless you are using a heavier than usual hook length material, this rig is more suited to the beach and estuary environment.

PARTS LIST

⇒   1 x Swivel.
⇒   1 x Three way swivel.
⇒   2 x Lead clip.
⇒   1 x Bait clip & tube.
⇒   1 x Bait shield & tube.
⇒   1 x Bead.
⇒   12 to 48" shockleader material.
⇒   24 to 96" Hook length material.
⇒   Stop knot material.
⇒   1 x hook 2/0 to 6/0

CLIPPED UP SINGLE

Clipped up rigs are normally used for distance casting and long range fishing in deeper water, the idea of the hooked bait being clipped towards the top of the rig is to stop worm baits etc. being blown up the hook length during the cast, this tends to happen quite a lot when casting long distances coupled with worm baits on standard paternoster type rigs.

One of the best weights to use with this rig is the one shown, a dumpy, this will allow the rig to roll around on the bottom, note there is no bottom swivel, this is not an oversight, using a bottom swivel actually cuts down and in some circumstances prevents the rig moving around.

PARTS LIST:

⇒ 1 x Swivel.
⇒ 1 x Three way swivel.
⇒ 1 x Bait clip & rubber tubing.
⇒ 1 x Hook size 1/0 to 6/0.
⇒ 1 x 18 inch Shockleader material.
⇒ 1 x 24 inch Shockleader material.
⇒ 1 x 18 inches hook length material.

As with most rigs the shockleader material used for the rig body should be the same or stronger than that used on your reel.

CLIPPED UP TWIN

Very different to the clipped up single the clipped up twin not only has two hook lengths but the bottom one is slightly longer than the lower rig body, this gives the angler two styles of fishing as the lower hook stays very close to the bottom.

This rig can however be adapted so that the lower hook stays slightly up in the water in the same way a paternoster works.

PARTS LIST:

⇒   1 x Swivel.
⇒   2 x Three way swivels.
⇒   2 x Bait clips & rubber tubing.
⇒   2 x Hook size 1/0 to 6/0.
⇒   1 x 18 inch Shockleader material.
⇒   1 x 24 inch Shockleader material.
⇒   1 x 12 inch Shockleader material.
⇒   1 x 14 inches hook length material.
⇒   1 x 18 inches hook length material.

This is a very good all round rig, but to move the baited hook off the sea bed simply reverse the two lower shockleader pieces so that the longer piece is at the bottom.

33

UP & OVER FLOUNDER RIG

This is basically the same as the previous rig with only two main differences, firstly the hook length has a number of brightly coloured beads on it, these act as an attractant and secondly the hook size, as flounder have relatively small mouths compared to most other species.

In this case the longer the rig/trace body the better the hook length will move around in the tidal flow.

It is good practice to either use a rig making board or a nail fixed in the wall to hang the rig body whilst fitting the hook length, if the later is used attach a weight to the end of the body, it will make things a little easier.

PARTS LIST

⇒   24 to 48" Shockleader material.
⇒   48 to 96" Hook length material.
⇒   1 x Size 1 to 2/0 hook.
⇒   1 x Bait clip & tube.
⇒   1 x Bait shield & tube.
⇒   1 x Swivel.
⇒   1 x Three way swivel.
⇒   2 x Lead clips/links.
⇒   Stop knot material, above bait shield bead.
⇒   Up to 12 Beads, various colours.
⇒   Note a crimp may be used instead of a stop knot.

34

SIMPLE RUNNING LEDGER SPINNING RIG

This light line rig is mainly used for flatfish, in slow moving currents in tidal estuaries, beads can be added to this rig as an attractor. This rig can also be used from the rocks and beach as a light spinning rig. The weight used is designed to run up and down the shockleader.

PARTS LIST

⇒   1 Barrel Lead 1.1-3ozs.
⇒   1 Bead. 1 Small Swivel.
⇒   18-24" Light Hook Length.1 Hook, Size 1-2/0.

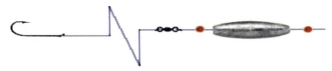

FLATFISH SNOOD

This beaded snood can be used on many different rigs, just by clipping it in place on the main rig body, directly to a swivel. The main use is for Plaice, Dab, Turbot and Flounder.

PARTS LIST

⇒   1 Snap Link. 1 Crimp. 6-12 Assorted Beads.
⇒   12-24" Of Hook Length. 1 Hook, Size 1-2/0.

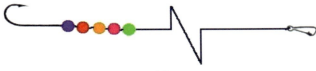

FLOUNDER RIG SINGLE

The flounder rig is very similar to the paternoster single with just a few modifications, first the bait shield and then the multi coloured beads on the hook length.

This rig is perfect for winter flounder fishing in estuaries around the united kingdom, but there is still room for improvement, simply by attaching to the lead end of the flounder twin via the lead link you have a triple hooked trace, however this is only possible if you follow the construction of the twin to the letter and use bait clips on the twin.

This rig will catch, with the right bait, flounder, plaice, whiting, cod, dab and mackerel.

PARTS LIST

⇒   24" of shockleader material.
⇒   12 to 18" Hook length material.
⇒   1 x size 1 to 2/0 BLN or Aberdeen hook.
⇒   1 x Three way swivel.
⇒   1 x Standard swivel.
⇒   1 x lead link/clip.
⇒   1 x Bait shield, tube and small bead.
⇒   Up to 12 various colour beads.
⇒   Stop knot material.
⇒   Note a crimp may be used in place of stop knot.

36

FLOUNDER RIG TWIN

Again this rig resembles the paternoster twin, but with a few modifications, if you intend to use this rig in conjunction with the flounder single you must use bait clips as a shield used on this rig will upset the casting balance and may cause a tangle of hook lengths, if however you intend to use this rig on it's own it is best to use a bait shield on the lower hook length.

When making this rig as with any other you must use the appropriate shockleader material to suit the lead being used, in the case of estuary fishing it is better to go up one level as you may find yourself using a heavier weight just to hold the rig to the bottom.

PARTS LIST

⇒   36" of appropriate shockleader material.
⇒   2 x 12 to 14" Hook length material.
⇒   2 x size 1 to 2/0 BLN or Aberdeen hooks.
⇒   2 x Three way swivels.
⇒   1 x Standard swivel.
⇒   1 x Lead clip/link.
⇒   2 x Bait clips and tube.
⇒   Up to 24 various coloured beads.

As with most rigs a lead link can be connected to the top of this rig for quick change should it be needed.

PENNEL HOOK SNOOD

This hook system can be used with most rigs by clipping it to a existing swivel and is mainly used for larger fish such as Bass, Cod, Pollack, Dogfish, Bull Huss and small Conger Eels. Please note this is attached to a paternoster single type rig.

PARTS LIST

⇒　1 Snap Link. 12-20" Of Heavy Hook Length.
⇒　1 Hook, Size 2/0-3/0. 1 Hook, Size 4/0-6/0.

WISHBONE SNOOD

This hook snood can be used in the same way as the Pennel snood, Built with medium to heavy line, this snood can be used for medium to long distance over slightly snaggy ground. Used for catching Bass, Cod, Whiting, Pollack, Bull Huss and dogfish.

PARTS LIST

⇒　1 Snap Link. 1 Medium to Heavy Swivel.
⇒　2 x 12" Medium Hook Lengths.
⇒　2 x Hook, Size 2/0-6/0.

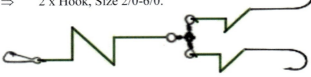

38

COALFISH SNOOD

This snood can be used, fished deep on a float system or on the bottom, on various other rigs. Placing a starlight in the piece of tube on this rig, helps to attract Coalfish, this snood works well fished after dark, for Scad also.

PARTS LIST

⇒   1 Snap Link. 1 Small to Medium swivel.
⇒   2 x Beads. 2 x Crimps. 1 Starlight and Tube.
⇒   12-20" Of Suitable Hook Length.1 Hook, Size 3/0.

BOTTOM RIG

This rig is mainly used for light bottom fishing, the hook length can be varied to suit casting and fish species, i.e. if the area to be fished has restricted room, then a shorter hook length should be used, however if fishing for Cod etc then this requires a longer trace.

PARTS LIST

⇒   1 Medium Swivel. 1 Three way Swivel. Lead Clip.
⇒   18-30" of Hook Length. 1 Hook, Size 1/0-6/0.

MPD SAND HUGGER SINGLE

The Mpd Sand hugger is designed to hold the bait on or just over the sea bed, it is in most respects a two piece rig set up as the barrel lead is placed onto the shockleader with a bead either side acting as a shock absorber against the leader knots, when using this set up you MUST NOT exceed 6ounces in total lead weight, the best combination is a 1 or 2ounce barrel and a 3 or 4ounce grip, the grip lead should be used as it acts as the main anchor for the entire rig.

This rig is mainly used for bottom feeders like Rays, Flattish etc, however Bass do take baits on this set up.

PARTS LIST:
⇒   1 x Barrel Lead.
⇒   2 x Beads.
⇒   1 x three way swivel.
⇒   1 x swivel.
⇒   1 x bait clip and tubing.
⇒   1 x Grip Lead
⇒   1 x Hook size 1/0 to 6/0.
⇒   1 x 8 inch shockleader material.
⇒   1 x 24 inch shockleader material.
⇒   1 x 18 inch Hook length material.

Remember the barrel lead must go on to the existing shockleader on the end of your mainline.

MPD SAND HUGGER TWIN

The Sand hugger rigs are ideally suited for the clean sandy beaches and estuaries, these also work very well from the boat and rock marks, however it is not recommended for use over rough ground.

The twin rig is slightly harder to cast, due to its length, however this can be adjusted to the anglers own specifications but if it is made too short it does have a habit of getting tangled.

These rigs work well with crab, worm and fish baits, use a wider beak hook for crab.

PARTS LIST:

⇒ 1 x Barrel Lead.
⇒ 2 x Beads.
⇒ 2 x three way swivel.
⇒ 1 x swivel.
⇒ 2 x bait clip and tubing.
⇒ 1 x Grip Lead
⇒ 2 x Hooks size 1/0 to 6/0.
⇒ 1 x 8 inch shockleader material.
⇒ 1 x 20 inch shockleader material.
⇒ 1 x 24 inch shockleader material.
⇒ 1 x 14 inch Hook length material.
⇒ 1 x 18 inch Hook length material.

As with the single rig the barrel slides up and down the shockleader.

The following four pieces of end tackle are normally used for catching flatfish, however these do work in cloudy water for most other species including Bass, Cod, Coalfish, Pollack, Whiting, Mackerel and so on.

The use of beads either plain coloured or illumines have been used for many years and have a tried and tested record, using these on other traces will almost certainly work with most species when the fishing is slow.

Spoons are another part in the tackle box that tend to be used when fishing for different members of flatfish, again, these can be used for attracting other species and work very well when spun for Mackerel, Pollack and Bass, try them you may just be surprised.

FLATFISH SPOON AND RIG

A variation of a normal flatfish rig, this set up can be used in slight currents and can also be retrieved slowly to help attract the fish. It is always best to
remember, to use smaller hooks for flatfish.

PARTS LIST

⇒ 1 Snap Link. 1 Small swivel. 1 Flatfish Spoon.
⇒ 1 Three Way Swivel. 1 Weight Clip.
⇒ 12-24" Of Shockleader
⇒ 10-18" Of Light Hook Length. 2 x Split Rings, these may be needed, if not supplied with spoon.

ATTRACTOR RIG

This rig can be purchased as one part, sometimes without the hook length. This rig is ideal for spinning worm baits across the bottom, mainly in estuaries. Mainly used for Flounder, this rig will catch other flatfish, with slight alterations to the hook and length.

PARTS LIST

⇒   1 Snap Link. 1 Crimp. 3-9 Beads. 1 Attractor Rig.
⇒   18" Of Light Hook Length. 1 Hook, Size 1-2/0.

SONAR TYPE ATTRACTOR

The spoon on this rig has slots cut out of it, this helps it to vibrate when it is retrieved through the water, and in doing so helps to attract the fish. This rig will work with most flatfish.

PARTS LIST

⇒   1 Snap Link. 3 Crimps. 6-10 Beads.
⇒   1 Sonar Attractor. 18" of Light Hook Length.
⇒   1 Flatfish Hook, Size 1-2/0.

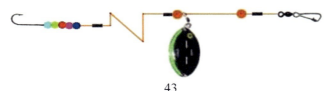

INLINE FLOUNDER SPOON

Purchased in one piece, these Flounder spoons will work with most flat fish, if the right bait is used.

It is often better to change the hook length and hook, these are normally short and the hooks can be blunt, in changing the hook length it is also possible to place coloured beads on this rig to act as an extra attractor.

PARTS LIST

⇒   1 Flounder Spoon. 12-18" Of Light Hook Length.
⇒   1 Crimp. 3-12 Coloured Beads. 1 x 1-2/0 hook.

The above spoon is one of many that can be purchased from angling centres around the United Kingdom, these come in a variety of shapes, patterns and weights.

Spoons are best used for spinning, whether its for flatfish, Mackerel or even Bass, spoons used correctly can be deadly for a number of species, as stated above the diagram it is better to remove any hook already attached and substitute it with a hook length and replacement hook.

This method also works very well from the boat, however substitute the hook length for a 6 to 12" wire trace line, if making this up yourself you will need small crimps to secure the spoon and hook length.

SPINNING RIG

This rig is mainly used for light spinning with rubber lures (Red Gills etc.) or Mackerel spinners, however this can also be used with live or frozen Sandeels. Cast out from beaches or the rocks this method can be deadly for Bass, Pollack, Mackerel, Scad and Garfish.

PARTS LIST

⇒   4 Beads. 2 bits silicon tubing. 2 x Small Swivels.
⇒   1 Barrel Weight to suit. 6-8" Of Shockleader.
⇒   12-24" Of Light Hook Length.
⇒   1 Rubber Sandeel etc. or 1 Hook, Size 2/0-3/0.

PLUGGING RIG

This is the easiest trace to make and is very basic, having a snap link at either end makes it easy to change plugs at a moments notice.

These can be purchased ready made up out of wire trace Material from most good angling shops see over page.

PARTS LIST

⇒   2 x Snap Links. 1 x Small Swivel.
⇒   24" light line/braid 8-12lbs, for use as the trace body.

READY MADE WIRE TRACE

These can be purchased from a wide range of angling shops and internet shops, they are available in a variety of lengths and breaking strains, if using one of these for spinning from the shore it is best to use the short light weight version.

HEAVY RUNNING LEDGER

This heavy running ledger is mainly used in conjunction with a heavy main line, and is tied directly to the shockleader at the swivel at the top of the trace. this is mainly used for fishing for Conger Eels.

PARTS LIST

⇒   2 x Heavy Swivels. 2 x Beads. 2 x Heavy Crimps.
⇒   1 Length Wire Trace Line. 1 Hook, Size 6/0-8/0.

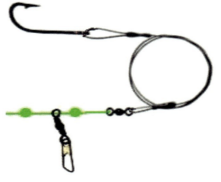

MACKEREL TRACE

Although this trace can be home made, it can be very time consuming, therefore it is probably best to purchase these from your local tackle dealer. This rig comes in many different forms, one of the more popular being the silver shrimp, these come in packs of three, four and six, if fishing in competition, only three hooks are allowed to be used as most rules state only three hooks are allowed in the water at any one time during competition.

Mackerel feathers can quite easily be made by the angler, however as they only cost a few pence to buy ready made it is better to but them from an angling shop, good angling suppliers have a wide range of mackerel feathers, silver shrimps and numerous other patterns to choose

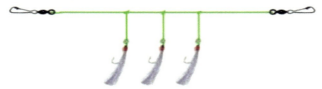

from. To make the above trace you will need to practice knot tying, first tie a swivel and clip on each end of 56" of shockleader material.

Now about 8" down the line make a loop of around 5" by tying a tucked half blood knot, then measure 8" again and repeat, do this for a third time and you should have a trace body of approximately 24 to 30".

Now cut one side of each of the loops, this should now

47

give you three hook lengths approximately 10" in length.

Once this has been done its time to decide whether or not you want beads, these are a good idea and the best ones to use are brightly coloured ones, however you will only need either one or two per hook length.

The material for the actual feather can be almost anything, however one of the best things that I have found to use that is plastic based and comes in a variety of colours from silver and gold through to metallic red, green, blue and even holographic is tinsel, this is very easy to work with and most households have it, if not you can purchase mixed packs for around a pound from many shopping outlets.

You now need to cut your tinsel or other material into lengths of around 3 to 4 inches, once done, to keep it all together use a very small amount of superglue, select your hook, in my case I will normally use a size 1/0 or 2/0 BLN, if these are unobtainable use the same sized Aberdeen hook.

Now comes the hard part, it can however be made easier with the use of either a match hook tyre, fly tying or small bench vice, with the beak of the hook held firmly use a dab of superglue to hold the tinsel in place running down the shank of the hook, now put the beads up the hook length and feed the free end through the eye of the hook, the reason for BLN or Aberdeen hooks are that the eye is just the right size for the following operations.

You need to push around 4.5 inches of the hook length

48

through the eye, now either tie a tucked half blood knot incorporating the hook shank or the easy method is to wrap the hook length around the hook shank and tinsel working down the hook towards the beak, do this up to 8 times, you can do less loops around the shank as long you do an even number it will still work, but the more loops/ twists you do the better it will hold.

Now still holding the free end push it back through the opposite side of the hook eye and pull up tight working the twists of line up the hook shank and tinsel as you go, you will note that some of the tinsel will pull up also, don't worry this is why the tinsel is the length it is.

When all is pulled up tight drop a dab of superglue in the eye of the hook, leave a few minutes to dry and then trim the tag of line left to around 5mm, trim the tinsel top level with the eye of the hook or lower if possible and then either trim the other end making sure that it passes the hook beak or leave long.

Now repeat on the other two hook lengths and remember as you are making your own you can change the pattern for each hook length.

Finally once finished hang from a nail or rig making board and then on each hook length take hold one strand of tinsel from the hook and holding firmly pull it through your nails of your fourth finger and thumb, you will notice that doing this will make the tinsel curl, do this on two or three strands only and if multi-coloured do one of each colour this will help cause vibrations when used and remember practice makes perfect.

DOWNTIDE RIG

When using a Downtide rig , there is no need for the use of a shockleader as you are not normally casting the weight but just lowering it over the side of the boat. This method of fishing accounts for many different species. The Weight used when downtiding can be very important, particularly if more than two people are using this If this is so then the best thing to do is , each person fishing uses a different sized weight, the lightest will drift the furthest downtide from the boat, the heavier the weight, the less the rig will drift, this should cut down on tangles between rigs from the same boat.

The shape of the weight is also important , plane leads work well, the best shape and most common is the cone shaped leads, these can be obtained in a variety of sizes.

PARTS LIST

⇒ 1 Large Zip Slider. 1 Large Bead, this acts as a buffer between the zip slider and swivel.

⇒ 2 x Large Swivels approximately size 1/0-4/0. 48" Of Heavy Line, From 25lbs to 50lbs.

⇒ 36" Of Heavy Line, for use as a hook length, Wire trace line can be used for larger species of fish.

⇒ 1 Hook, Size 3/0-6/0.

UPTIDE RIG

This method of fishing is a fairly new technique compared with Downtiding, the term Uptiding is exactly what it sounds like. with this method of fishing a shockleader may be needed depending on the size of weight and strength of main line being used. The use of grip leads are very important with this method. The idea of uptiding is to cast a weighted rig from the boat so that the lead settles on the bottom , uptide from the boat, and the baited trace moves with the tide. with this method of fishing, if there are three or more anglers on the boat, a larger area of ground can be covered. This method accounts for many species of fish, as does the downtide rig. The Pennel type hook trace on this rig is optional and works well for the larger species of fish. The clip on this rig is for changing the hook length, to suit different conditions and different species of fish. This type of rig is a type of running ledger.

PARTS LIST

⇒   1 Sliding Boom, Although a Zip Slider can be used. 1 Large Bead to act as a buffer.
⇒   2 Large Swivels Size 1/0 to 4/0. 1 Clip Link or Snap Link. 1 x 3/0 - 6/0 Hook
⇒   18-24" Of Heavy Line, for use as a hook length.
⇒   1 x 3/0 and 1 x 5/0 hook, if using a Pennel Rig.

COD RIG

The Cod is the most popular and sought after winter fish to be caught from the boat, although there are numerous ways and rigs for catching this fish, the rig above is one of the more popular ones. This rig can be used in two or three ways, these are, 1, to lower the baited rig over the side of the boat with a large weight and drift the rig over wrecks and reefs. 2, With the boat anchored lower the baited rig over the side with a 6-8oz lead and use as if downtiding. 3, With the boat anchored, cast the baited rig complete with a grip lead of 6 - 8ozs up tide from the boat, when this settles on the bottom, periodically release a few feet of line off of the reel. If the latter of the methods are used, there may be a need to use a shockleader, depending on the strength of the main line used. This rig will work with a variety of species particularly Pollack and Ling, by changing the trace line, hook size and bait this rig will work with Conger Eels.

PARTS LIST

1 Medium Eddystone Boom. 1 Large Bead, (2 Beads are used if a shockleader is used with this trace). 1 Large Swivel, Size 1/0 - 2/0. Up To 72" Of Trace Line, Average Size Around 30lbs. 1 Hook, Size 6/0 - 8/0, depending on species. A Pennel Hook can be used with this rig.

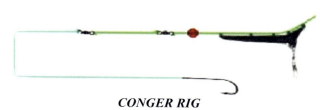

CONGER RIG

This rig set-up is very similar to the Cod rig, however this rig uses heavier line larger hooks and more swivels. Conger fishing from the boat is normally done by, anchoring the boat over a wreck or reef and lowering the baited rig (normally with a whole Mackerel or flapper) over the side, until it reaches the bottom, this can be left where it is, or the reel can be turned two or three turns to raise the boom off the bottom and away from any under water snags, doing this may let the rig drift, however this will cover a larger area. This rig will often attract Ling and other species of smaller fish, before striking in to the fish, be certain that the bite is sharp or is pulling line off the reel. Up to a 2lb plane weight may be needed for this rig, and a main line of 50lbs plus. When boat fishing for larger species, always make sure that the drag is set properly on the reel, to do this, loosen the drag until line can be pulled from the reel, without snapping, the line should not run off the reel freely.

PARTS LIST

⇒ 1 Large Eddystone Boom. 1 Large Bead.
⇒ 2 x Swivels, Size 3/0 - 4/0. 1 x Hook size 8/0.
⇒ 24" Of 200lb Mono, between swivels.
⇒ 48" Of Wire Trace Line or 200lbs mono.

POLLACK RIG

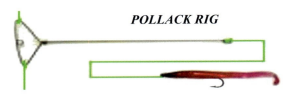

This rig is one of the more popular ones, and is used for a variety of other species of fish, used mainly by lowering the baited rig (with a rubber sand eel) over the side of the boat until the weight hits the bottom, once this has happened turn the reel between 6 and 10 turns to raise the rig off of the bottom, this is about the area in which Pollack swim and feed, however other fish such as Ling and Cod also occupy this area. Another method that can be used with this rig is to put a flier at the top of the trace, this helps to attract fish towards the rig and ultimately the rubber eel with the hook inserted in it. Rubber eels come in a variety of shapes and sizes, the way that a flier is set-up is to push the trace line through a smaller eel and then push it up to the end of the boom. The most productive being the red and black ones.

PARTS LIST

⇒   1 x 8 - 10" Wire Boom.
⇒   20lb Trace Line, Approximately 15 feet.
⇒   1 Large Rubber eel (redgill/ eddyston. Etc.)

Jelly worms also work on this rig and are worth a try if the fishing is slow.

TOPE RIG

This rig can be used with a grip lead as shown for uptiding or with a plane lead for down tiding, although mainly used for tope fishing, this rig can be used for a variety of fish by changing the hook size and weight. When using this rig it is not unusual to use a whole Mackerel for bait, the tope can take and swallow a whole fish in one gulp. This fish is widely distributed and is found over clean sand, shingle bottoms. Please note that the Tope is a protected species and as such a catch and return policy should be adopted.

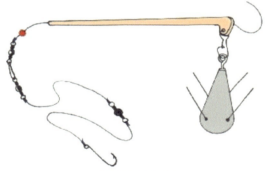

PARTS LIST

⟹ 1 Sliding Boom, Zip slider can be substituted
⟹ 1 Large Bead used as a buffer.
⟹ 3 Large Swivels size 1/0 - 4/0.
⟹ 48" Of 50lb Line for use as a rubbing Trace.
⟹ 12-24" Of Heavy Wire Trace Line or 60lb Mono.
⟹ 2 x Heavy Gauge Crimps, if Wire Trace line is used.
⟹ 1 Hook, Size 7/0 and up.

FEATHERED AND PLANE PIRKING RIG

This rig setup is very common, and is used mainly for Cod etc. The feathers on the rig at the top of the page can be of any colour, however the most commonly used and most popular are the white ones. Pirks come in many shapes and sizes normally between 8 and 16ozs.

Pirk fishing is normally carried out when the boat is drifting over a reef or wreck. A good method is to lower the Pirk, baited with a whole squid, over the side till it reaches the bottom, then retrieve the Pirk about 7 turns of the reel to clear any snags, now raise the rod tip and then lower it. This is done until the fish are contacted and hooked. Basic Pirks are made from a piece of stainless steel tube, filled with lead, however it is probably best to purchase ready made ones from a local tackle dealer.

PARTS LIST

⇒   1 Set Of Cod Feathers.
⇒   1 Large 2/0 - 4/0 Swivel.
⇒   35lb Main Line.
⇒   1 Pirk Between 8 and 6ozs.

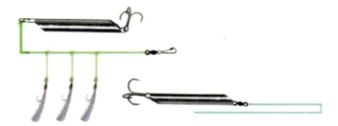

Printed in France by Amazon
Brétigny-sur-Orge, FR

18775704R00033